THIS BOOK BELONGS TO

Greg Adams

Published by Longmeadow Press, 201 High Ridge Road, Stamford, Connecticut 06904. ISBN 0-681-40333-0. Printed in the U.S.A. 0 9 8 7 6 5 4 3 2 1

Where in the World Is Walter?

A Book of Discovery

By Don Ross
and
Sue Levytsky
Illustrated by Don Ross

Longmeadow Press

"Where am I?"
said Walter Muttson.

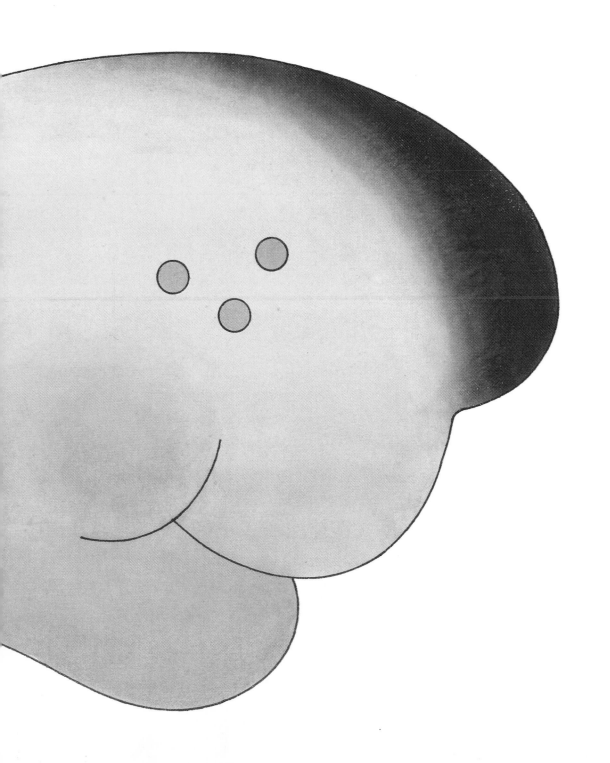

"You're in your bed, Walter," said his mother.
"Where's my bed?" he asked.

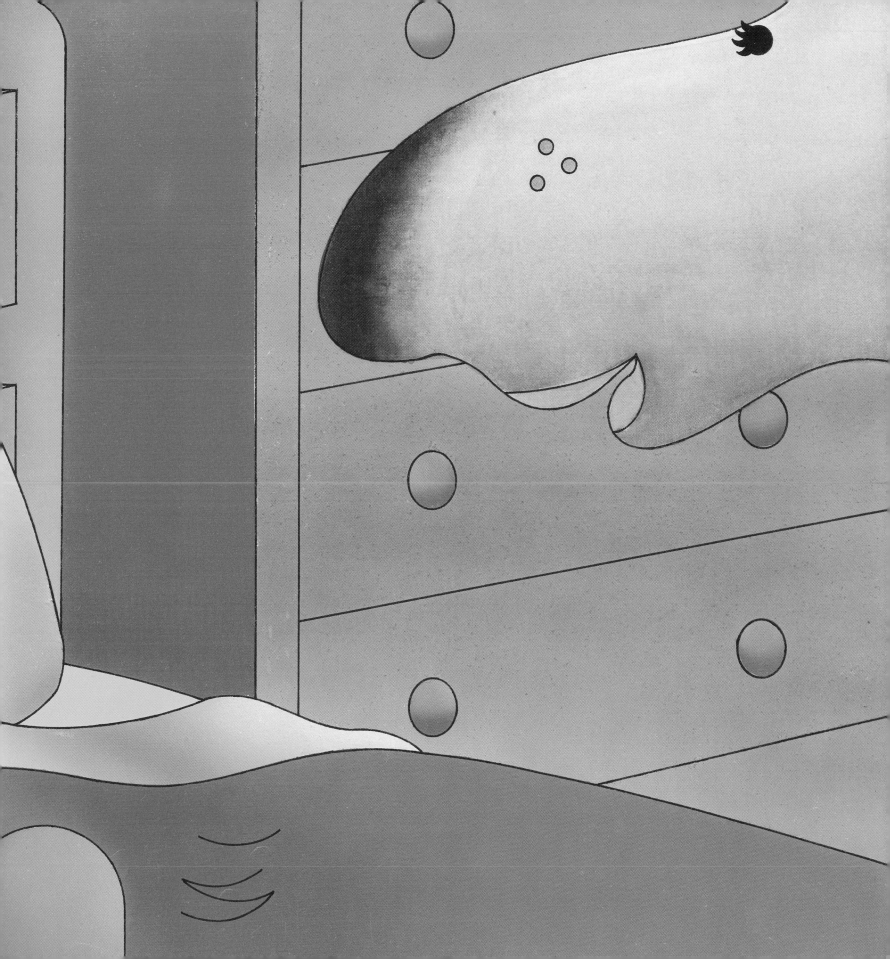

"It's in your room," his mother replied
as she tucked him in for a nap.

"Where's my room, Mom?"

"It's in your house, Walter."
"I'm in my bed. I'm in my room.
I'm in my house," said Walter.
"But where's my house?"

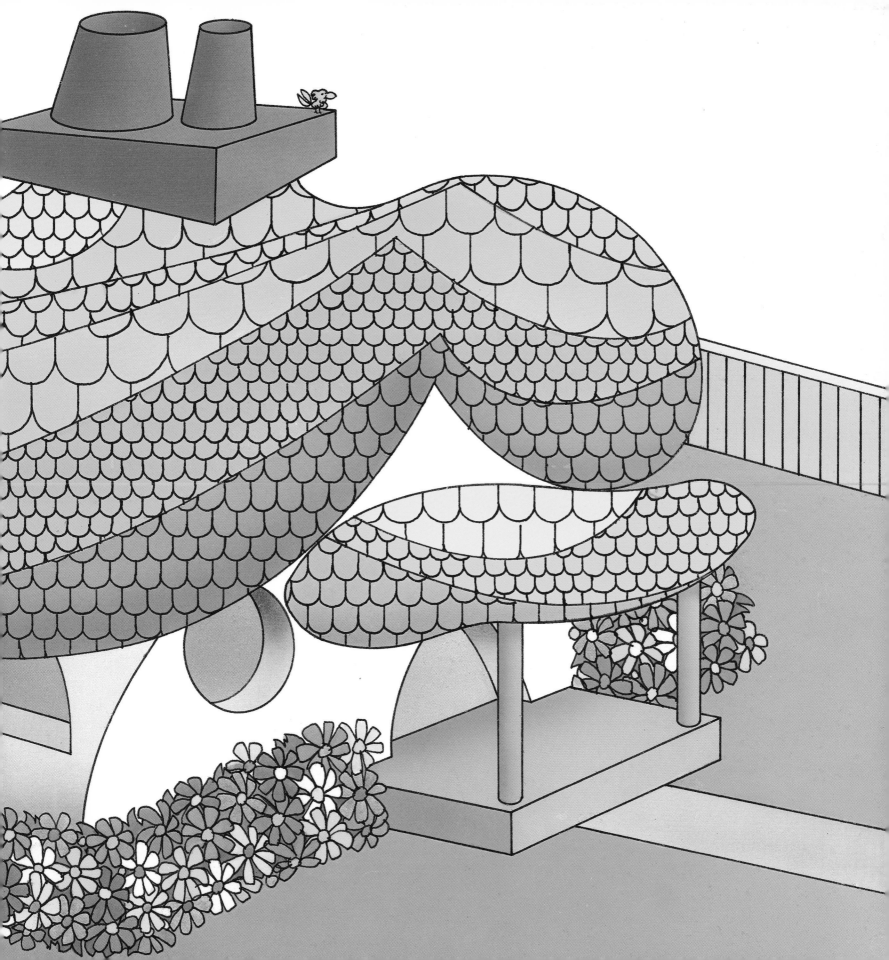

"Your house is on your street," said his mother, "along with all your neighbors' houses." Walter wanted to know even more. "Where's my street?" he asked.

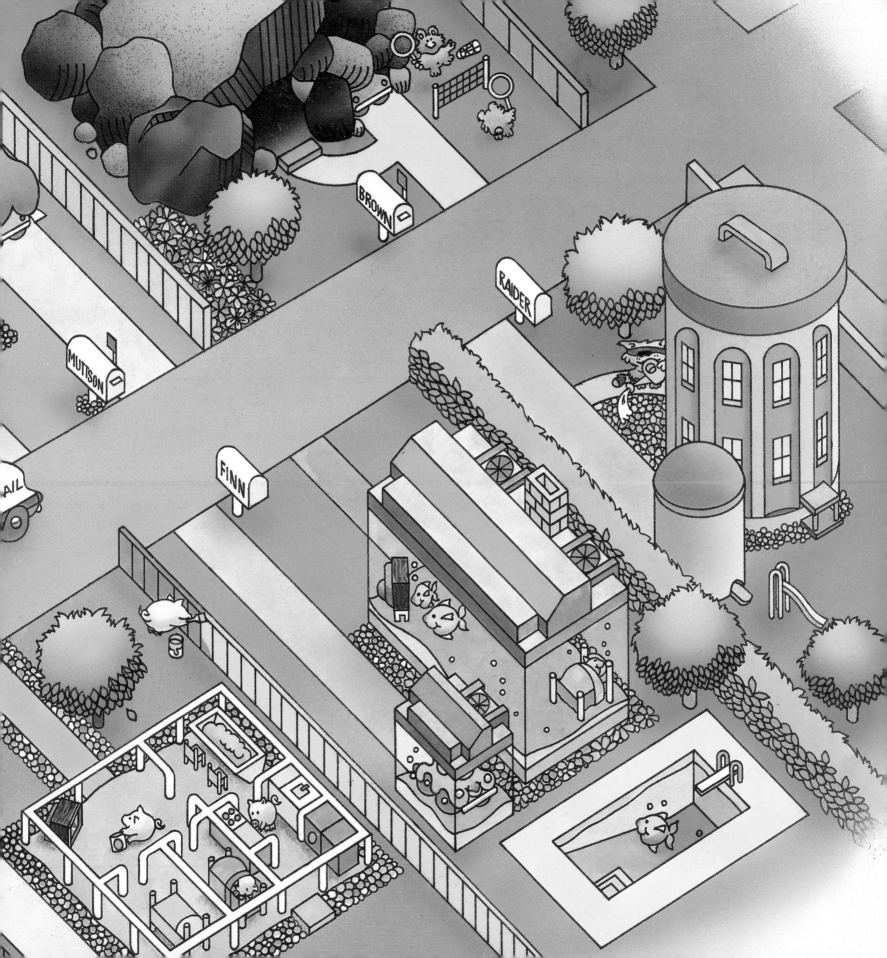

"It's in your town, Tailwag," his mother explained.

"Gee. I'm in lots of places at the same time.

I'm in my bed.
I'm in my room.
I'm in my house.
I'm on my street.
My street is in my town.

Mom, where's my town?"

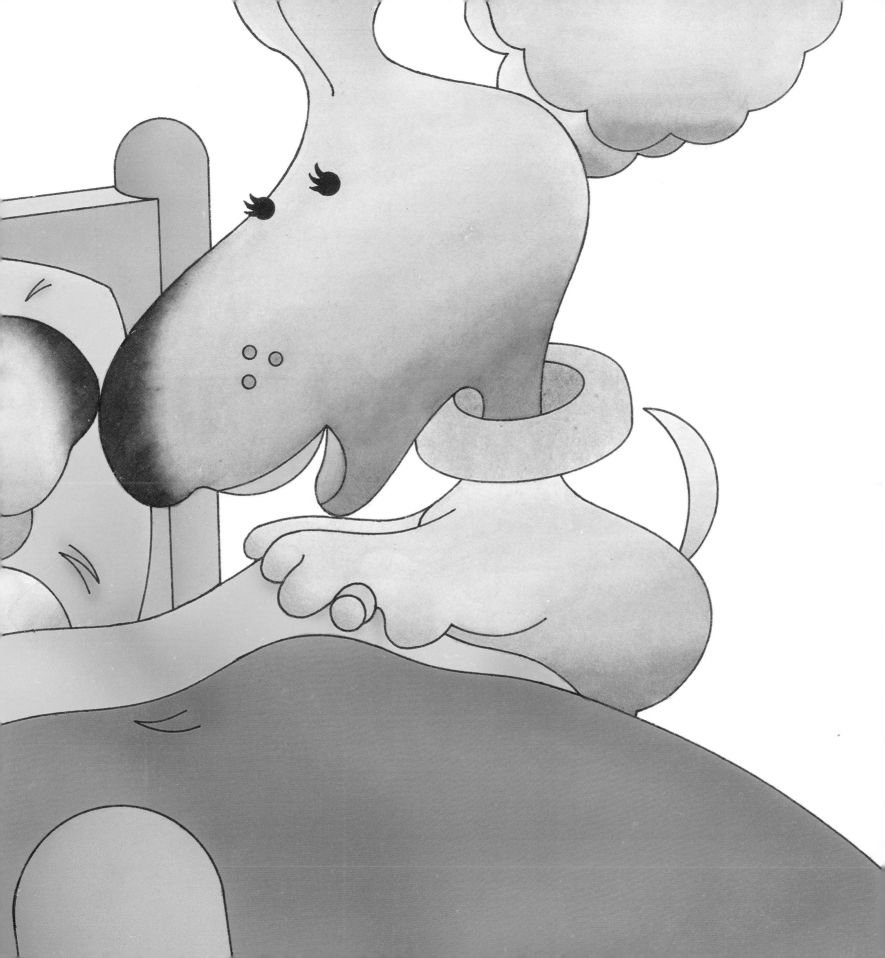

"Your town is in your state,"
Walter's mother replied.

"Where's my state?"
asked Walter.

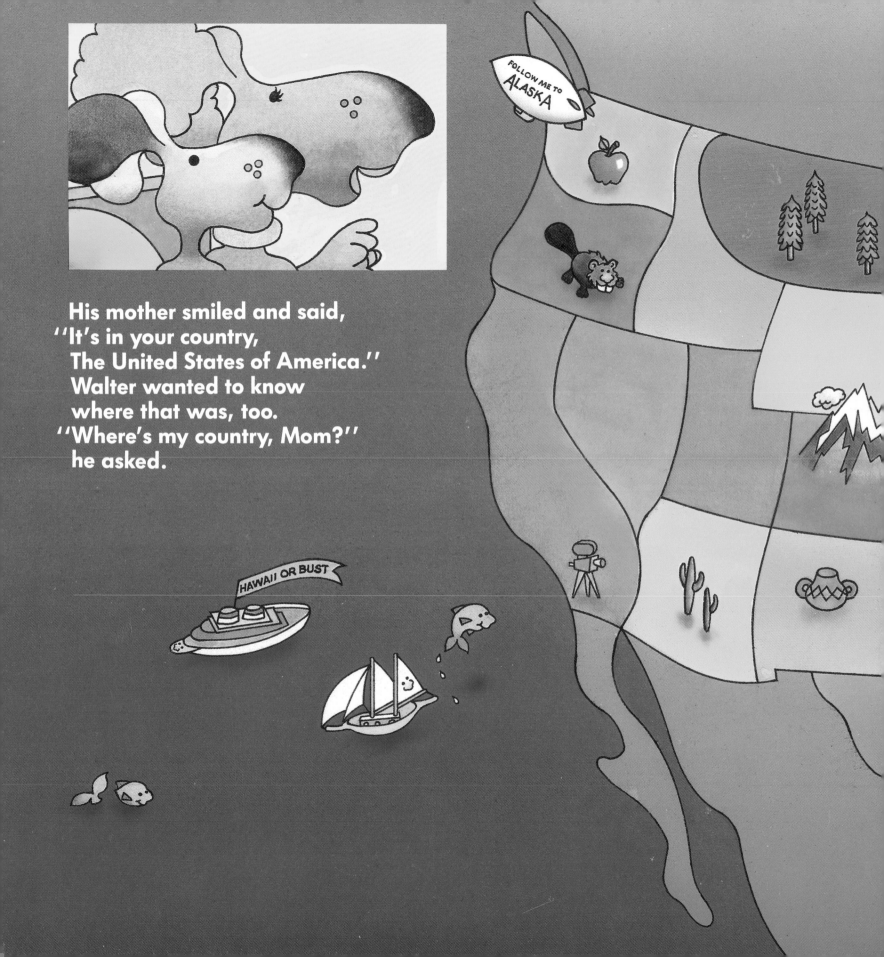

His mother smiled and said,
"It's in your country,
The United States of America."
Walter wanted to know
where that was, too.
"Where's my country, Mom?"
he asked.

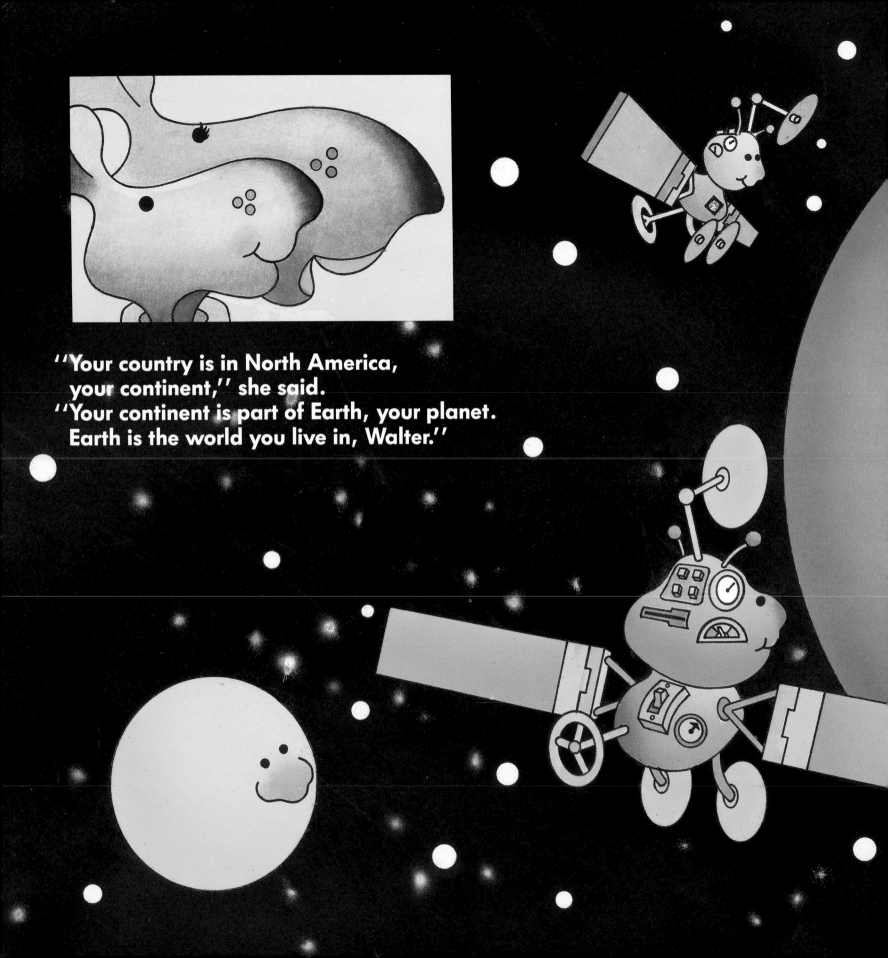

"Your country is in North America,
   your continent," she said.
"Your continent is part of Earth, your planet.
   Earth is the world you live in, Walter."

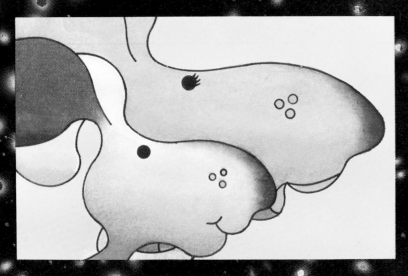

"But Earth is also part of the universe,
along with all the other planets
and stars and galaxies in the sky."
"I'm in so many places," said Walter.
"I'm in the universe.
I'm on Earth.
I'm in my country.
I'm in my state and in my town.
I'm on my street and in my house.
I'm in my room.
I'm in my bed and..."

"...here in my arms with me,"
said his mother as she
gave him a great big hug.
And Walter knew that was
the best place of all to be.